THIS WALKER BOOK BELONGS TO:

_____

_____

_____

_____

To
"The Adventurers"

Wild Thing (Harry),
Butler (Naomi),
Peanut (Beth) and
Krispy (Krissy)

– for the wild adventures
we've had and the ones we've
yet to encounter...

And to Helen – my warmest thanks.

First published 1999 by Walker Books Ltd
87 Vauxhall Walk, London SE11 5HJ

This edition published 2000

2 4 6 8 10 9 7 5 3

This book has been typeset in Garamond ITC Book Condensed.

Printed in Hong Kong

British Library Cataloguing in Publication Data
A catalogue record for this book is
available from the British Library.

ISBN 0-7445-7799-3

Days Like This

a collection of small poems
selected and illustrated by

Simon James

WALKER BOOKS
AND SUBSIDIARIES
LONDON • BOSTON • SYDNEY

The Adventurers

We love adventures,
Where we live is
anybody's guess.

We love the open land
and the open land
is our address.

Simon James

Stepping Stones

Stepping over stepping stones, one, two, three,
Stepping over stepping stones, come with me.
The river's very fast
And the river's very wide
And we'll step across on stepping stones
And reach the other side.

Traditional

A Lazy Thought

There go the grownups
To the office,
To the store.
Subway rush,
Traffic crush;
Hurry, scurry,
Worry, flurry.

No wonder
Grownups
Don't grow up
Any more.

It takes a lot
Of slow
To grow.

Eve Merriam

The Guppy

Whales have calves,
Cats have kittens,
Bears have cubs,
Bats have bittens;
Swans have cygnets,
Seals have puppies,
But guppies just have
little guppies.

Ogden Nash

Sledging

Look at us

As we go

Sledging on the bright white snow.

Faces beaming

Long hair streaming

Passing those who are too slow.

Wendy Elizabeth Johnson

15

On My Little Guitar

On my little guitar
With only one string
I play in the moonlight
Any old thing.

C. Louis Leipoldt

Rain

Rain on the green grass,
And rain on the tree;
And rain on the housetop,
But not upon me.

Traditional

Tomorrow

Tomorrow's never there.
It always runs away.
Every time I catch it
It says it's called Today.

Steve Turner

The Picnic

We brought a rug for sitting on,
Our lunch was in a box.
The sand was warm. We didn't wear
Hats or Shoes or Socks.

Waves came curling up the beach.
We waded. It was fun.
Our sandwiches were different kinds.
I dropped my jammy one.

Dorothy Aldis

The Wind Came Running

The Wind came running
over the sand,
it caught and held me
by the hand.

It curled and whirled
and danced with me
down to the edge
of the dashing sea.

We danced together,
the Wind and I,
to the cry of a gull
and a wild sea cry.

Ivy O. Eastwick

First Day at School

My first day at school to-day.
Funny sort of day.
Didn't seem to learn much.
Seemed all we did was play.

Then teacher wrote some letters
On a board all painted black,
And then we had a story and …
I don't think I'll go back.

Rod Hull

Sleeping Outdoors

Under the dark
is a star,
Under the star
is a tree,
Under the tree
is a blanket,
And under the blanket
is me.

Marchette Chute

The Summer Sun

Yes,
The sun shines bright
In the summer,
And the breeze is soft
As a sigh.

Yes,
The days are long
In the summer,
And the sun is king
Of the sky.

Wes Magee

The Seed

How does it know,
this little seed,
if it is to grow
to a flower or weed,

if it is to be
a vine or shoot,
or grow to a tree
with a long deep root?

A seed is so small
where do you suppose
it stores up all
of the things it knows?

Aileen Fisher

Bouncing

My mum,
bounce,
doesn't like it.
My dad,
bounce,
goes out of his head.
But I love to bounce,
bounce, bounce
on top of my bed.

My mum,
bounce,
calls out.
My dad,
bounce,
shouts from the hall.
But when I'm bouncing,
bouncing, bouncing,
I take no
bounce
notice at all.

Simon James

Pink Azalea

I feel as though
this bush were grown
especially for me.

I feel as though
I almost am
this little flowering tree.

Charlotte Zolotow

Two in Bed

When my brother Tommy
Sleeps in bed with me
He doubles up
And makes
himself
exactly
like
a
V
And 'cause the bed is not so wide
A part of him is on my side.

Abram Bunn Ross

My Love For You

I know you little,
I love you lots.
My love for you
Would fill ten pots,
Fifteen buckets,
Sixteen cans,
Three teacups
And four dishpans.

Traditional

Today

Yesterday has gone
Tomorrow's yet to be,
Today is now
and always here
For everyone to see.

Simon James

Index of Titles

A Lazy Thought by Eve Merriam 10

Bouncing by Simon James 35

First Day at School by Rod Hull 26

My Love For You Traditional 40

On My Little Guitar by C. Louis Leipoldt 17

Pink Azalea by Charlotte Zolotow 36

Rain Traditional 18

Sledging by Wendy Elizabeth Johnson 15

Sleeping Outdoors by Marchette Chute 28

Stepping Stones Traditional 9

The Adventurers by Simon James 6

The Guppy by Ogden Nash 12

The Picnic by Dorothy Aldis 22

The Seed by Aileen Fisher 32

The Summer Sun by Wes Magee 30

The Wind Came Running by Ivy O. Eastwick 25

Today by Simon James 42

Tomorrow by Steve Turner 20

Two in Bed by Abram Bunn Ross 38

ACKNOWLEDGEMENTS

The publisher would like to thank the copyright holders for permission to reproduce the following: "A Lazy Thought" from *There Is No Rhyme for Silver* by Eve Merriam. Copyright © 1962, © renewed 1990 Eve Merriam. By permission of Marian Reiner; "First Day at School" from *The Reluctant Pote* copyright © 1983 Rod Hull. Reproduced by permission of Hodder and Stoughton Limited; "On My Little Guitar" by C. Louis Leipoldt, translated by A. Delius. Reprinted by kind permission of Dr Peter Shields; "Pink Azalea" from *River Winding* copyright © 1970 Charlotte Zolotow. Reprinted by permission of S©ott Treimel New York for the author; "Sleeping Outdoors" from *Rhymes About Us* by Marchette Chute. Published 1974 by E.P. Dutton. Copyright © 1974 Marchette Chute. Reprinted by permission of Elizabeth Roach; "The Guppy" reprinted by permission of Curtis Brown, Ltd. Copyright © 1944 Ogden Nash, renewed; "The Picnic" from *Hop, Skip and Jump!* by Dorothy Aldis. Copyright © 1934, © renewed 1961 Dorothy Aldis. Used by permission of G.P. Putnam's Sons, a division of Penguin Putnam Inc.; "The Seed" from *Up the Windy Hill* by Aileen Fisher. Copyright © 1953 Aileen Fisher, © renewed 1981 Aileen Fisher. Used by permission of Marian Reiner for the author; "The Summer Sun" by Wes Magee, from *Dragon Smoke: Poetry One* (Basil Blackwell, 1985). Copyright © 1985 Wes Magee. By permission of the author; "The Wind Came Running" by Ivy O. Eastwick from *Cherry Stones! Garden Swings!* by Ivy O. Eastwick. Copyright © 1962 Abingdon Press. Used by permission; "Tomorrow" copyright © 1996 Steve Turner. First published in *The Day I Fell Down the Toilet and Other Poems* (Lion 1996). Reprinted by kind permission of the author and Lisa Eveleigh; "The Adventurers", "Bouncing" and "Today" are copyright © 1999 Simon James. Every effort has been made to obtain permission to reproduce copyright material but there may be cases where we have been unable to trace a copyright holder. The publisher will be happy to correct any omission in future printings.

Days Like This

SIMON JAMES says of *Days Like This*, "When I was invited to do this book, it was just going to be another anthology. But as I began collecting poems, I kept finding little gems crammed in on a page and realized they needed room to be heard and seen." The smallness of the poems is also suited to the feeling of intimacy and spontaneity that lies at the heart of all his work. As he explains, "I like to capture a large world and at the same time give the reader the sense of being drawn into an intimate moment or place."

Simon is an award-winning author and illustrator of books for children, and a regular speaker in schools and at festivals across the UK and the US. His books for Walker include *My Friend Whale*, *Sally and the Limpet*, *The Wild Woods* and *Leon and Bob*, for which he won the Smarties Book Prize Silver Medal and the New York Times Best Illustrated Book of the Year. He lives in south Devon.

ISBN 0-7445-2349-4 (pb)

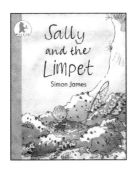

ISBN 0-7445-2020-7 (pb)

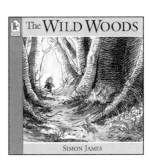

ISBN 0-7445-3661-8 (pb)

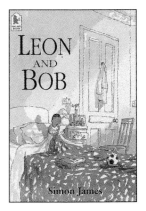

ISBN 0-7445-5491-8 (pb)